SI ONLINE

Multimedia Resources for
**TEACHERS
STUDENTS
PARENTS**

SOUND INNOVATIONS

W9-BZQ-566

for CONCERT BAND

A Revolutionary Method for Beginning Musicians

Robert **SHELDON** | Peter **BOONSHAFT** | Dave **BLACK** | Bob **PHILLIPS**

Congratulations on deciding to be a member of the band!

This book is here to help you get started on a very exciting time in your life. When you complete Book 1, you'll be well prepared to play many types and styles of music. Playing in the band will bring you years of incredible experiences.

Maybe you'll make music an important part of your life by attending concerts, playing in a community band, and supporting the arts. Maybe you'll pursue a career in music as a performer, teacher, composer, sound engineer, or conductor. Whatever you choose, we wish you the best of luck in becoming a part of the wonderful world of music.

Correlated *Sound Innovations* media will help you practice and develop new skills. Video lessons and audio demonstration tracks reinforce good technique and musical accuracy, and PDFs provide supplemental tunes, exercises, lessons, and assessment pages. Visit the *SI Online* resource site for access:

SIOnline.alfred.com

SI ONLINE

Multimedia Resources for
**TEACHERS
STUDENTS
PARENTS**

🔊 Audio demonstration and accompaniment tracks are included for every line of music in the book.

🎥 Video demonstrations of fundamental skills and exercises are included. Look for the video icon throughout this book.

📄 Supplemental enrichment content and additional repertoire for practice and reinforcement are available to download at SIOnline.alfred.com.

Visit the *SI Online* resource site to stay up to date with newly added content.
SIOnline.alfred.com

Alfred Music
P.O. Box 10003
Van Nuys, CA 91410-0003
alfred.com

ISBN-10: 0-7390-6733-8 (Book & Online Media)
ISBN-13: 978-0-7390-6733-8 (Book & Online Media)

Instrument photos courtesy of Yamaha Corporation of America Band & Orchestral Division
Audio recorded and mixed at The Lodge Recording Studios, Indianapolis, IN
Trombone performance in audio recordings by Loy Hetrick
Accompaniments written and recorded by Derek Richard
All ensembles, including *Sound Innovations Fanfare*, performed by American Symphonic Winds, Anthony Maiello, Conductor

Production Company: Specialized Personnel Locators
Engineer: Kendall S. Thomsen
Video filming and production: David Darling, Grand Haven, MI
Trombone artist in video: Joseph Rodriguez

Ready? Set? Play!
Sound advice for getting started on your instrument

1. YOUR INSTRUMENT—PARTS OF THE TROMBONE

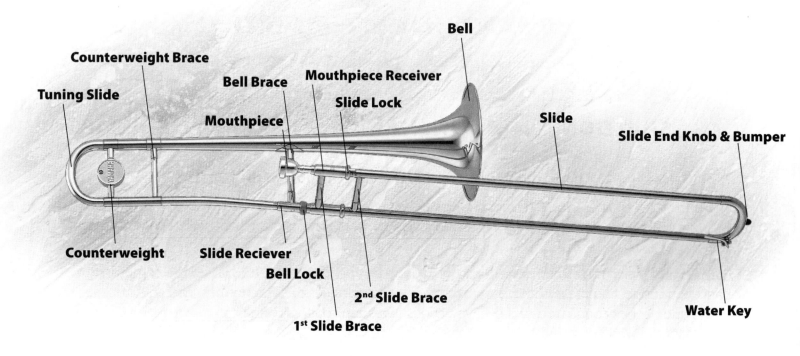

2. PUTTING IT ALL TOGETHER

A. Make sure the slide is locked.

B. Carefully hold the bell-half of the trombone with your left hand and the slide-half with your right.

C. Position the slide at a 90 degree angle in the slide receiver and tighten the bell lock.

D. Hold the instrument in your left hand and carefully place the mouthpiece in the mouthpiece receiver.

E. Gently twist the mouthpiece to the right being careful not to over tighten.

F. Lubricate the slide regularly. There are several ways to lubricate the slide. Your teacher will demonstrate how to do this. Clean your hands after applying.

D. Grease the tuning slide regularly being careful not to dent or bend the slide. Wipe off excess slide grease and clean your hands after applying.

▶ *Instrument Assembly*
▶ *Disassembly*
▶ *Oiling the Slide*
▶ *Care & Maintenance*

3. PUTTING IT ALL AWAY

A. Remove the mouthpiece by gently twisting it to the left and place it in the mouthpiece holder in the case.

B. If your mouthpiece gets stuck, seek help from your teacher or a music dealer. They have a special tool to remove a stuck mouthpiece that will not damage the instrument.

C. Press the water key and gently blow air through the mouthpiece receiver to remove excess condensation on to a soft cloth or the floor.

D. Wipe off the outside with a soft cloth. Carefully place the instrument in the case and close all the latches.

E. Store only your instrument and its accessories in the case. Music, folders and other objects may bend or dent the slide and damage the instrument.

First Sounds

POSTURE AND PLAYING POSITION

A. Sit on the front edge of the chair.

B. Keep feet flat on the floor.

C. Sit tall with your back straight.

D. Hold the trombone with your left hand.

E. Place your left thumb around the bell brace.

F. Place your left index finger on the mouthpiece receiver.

G. Wrap your other fingers naturally around the first slide brace.

H. Your left hand holds the weight of the trombone.

I. Place your right thumb and first two fingers on the second slide brace to move the slide.

J. Keep your right hand, wrist, elbow and shoulder relaxed and flexible.

EMBOUCHURE

A. Your mouth position (or embouchure) is an important part of creating a good sound.

B. Moisten your lips and bring them together as if saying the letter "M."

C. Keeping your jaw open and relaxed, pull back the corners of your mouth to form a puckered smile.

D. The corners of your lips should stay firm while the lips stay relaxed.

E. Place the mouthpiece so that it's directly centered on your lips.

BREATHING

A. Take a full breath by inhaling deeply through your mouth

B. Exhale gently and completely.

C. Neck and shoulders should be relaxed. Shoulders should not move, but the waist should expand with each breath.

PLAYING YOUR FIRST SOUNDS

A. Use only the mouthpiece to begin making a sound.

B. Form your embouchure on the mouthpiece.

C. Take a deep, full breath through the corners of your mouth.

D. Buzz and exhale through the mouthpiece while you say "tah." Hold the note as long as possible. Also buzz your lips without the mouthpiece.

E. Play several sounds on one breath by saying, "tah, tah, tah." This is called "tonguing" since you are using your tongue to start the new sound.

F. Make a "siren" sound on the mouthpiece, making the sound go up and down smoothly by changing the size in the opening in the middle of your lips.

EQUIPMENT NEEDS

A. Keep slide lubricant and slide grease in your case for maintaining your instrument.

B. Use a soft, clean cloth to wipe off the outside of the trombone prior to storage.

▶ *Posture*

▶ *Breathing*

▶ *Hands & Fingers*

▶ *Embouchure & First Sounds*

▶ *Tonguing*

Sound Notation

Music has its own language and symbols that are recognized worldwide.

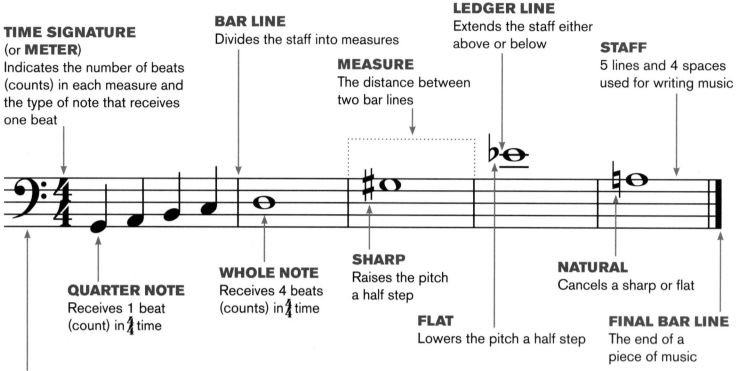

TIME SIGNATURE
(or **METER**)
Indicates the number of beats (counts) in each measure and the type of note that receives one beat

BAR LINE
Divides the staff into measures

MEASURE
The distance between two bar lines

LEDGER LINE
Extends the staff either above or below

STAFF
5 lines and 4 spaces used for writing music

QUARTER NOTE
Receives 1 beat (count) in ¼ time

WHOLE NOTE
Receives 4 beats (counts) in ¼ time

SHARP
Raises the pitch a half step

FLAT
Lowers the pitch a half step

NATURAL
Cancels a sharp or flat

FINAL BAR LINE
The end of a piece of music

BASS CLEF
Also called F clef (the 4th line of the staff is F and the clef is drawn by starting on the F Line) and includes a dot above and below the F line

---

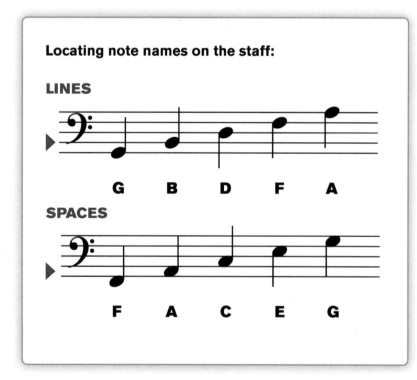

Locating note names on the staff:

LINES

G B D F A

SPACES

F A C E G

HOW TO PRACTICE

As you play through this book, some parts will be very easy while others may require more time to play well. Practicing your instrument every day will help you achieve excellence. Carefully play each exercise until you can perform it comfortably three times in succession.

▶ Practice in a quiet place where you can concentrate.

▶ Schedule a regular practice time every day.

▶ Use a straight back chair and a music stand to assist you in maintaining good posture.

▶ Start each practice session by warming up on low notes and long tones.

▶ Focus on the music that is most difficult to play, then move on to that which is easier and more fun.

▶ Use your recordings to help you play in tune and in time.

🎥 ▶ *A Good Tone*

🔊 1 Listen to the note and match the pitch. This is the first note you learn on page 5.

Level 1: Sound Beginnings 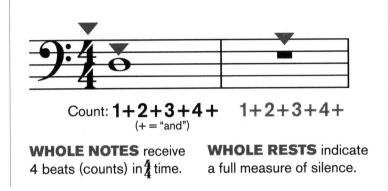 ▶ *First Five Notes*

The **BASS CLEF** (F Clef) identifies the location of notes on the staff. The two dots of the bass clef are above and below the F on the staff. F is on the 4th line.

A **TIME SIGNATURE** or **METER** indicates the number of beats (counts) in each measure and the kind of note that receives one beat.

$\frac{4}{4}$ **TIME** is a meter in which there are 4 beats per measure and the quarter note receives 1 beat.

Count: **1+2+3+4+**   **1+2+3+4+**
(+ = "and")

WHOLE NOTES receive 4 beats (counts) in $\frac{4}{4}$ time.

WHOLE RESTS indicate a full measure of silence.

OUR FIRST NOTE *Introducing the new note, D.*

2

1+2+3+4+   1+2+3+4+

OUR SECOND NOTE *Introducing the new note, C.*

3

TWO-NOTE TANGO—*Practice going from one note to the other.*

4

OUR THIRD NOTE *Introducing the new note, B♭.*

5

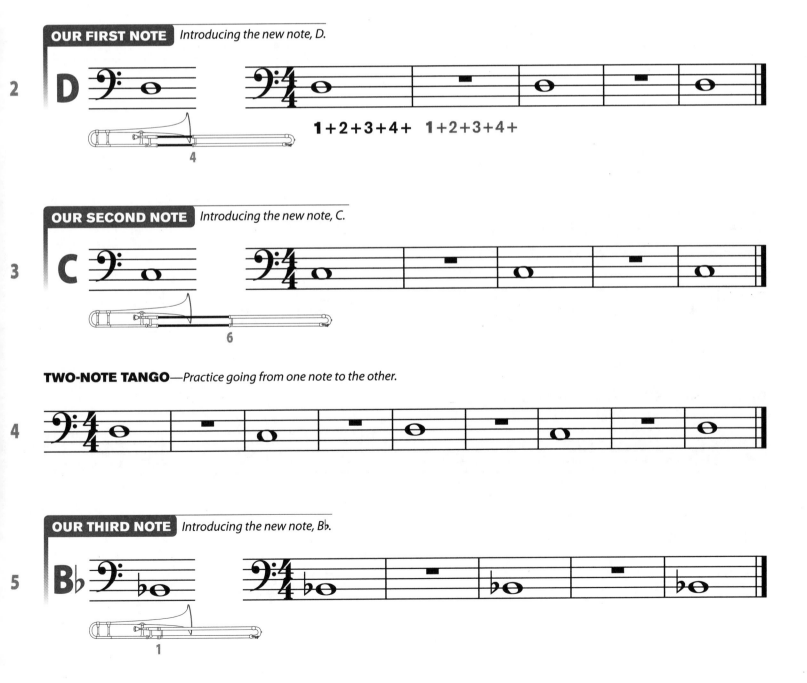

THREE-NOTE COMBO—*Practice playing all three notes.*

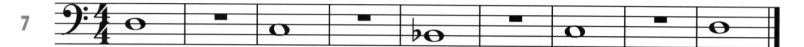

THIRD TIME'S THE CHARM—*Additional practice on these three notes.*

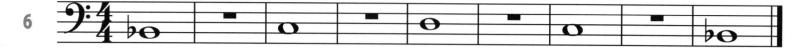

A **SOLO** is when one person is performing alone or with accompaniment.

MATCH THE PITCH—*Play the solo part as the rest of the band answers with the same note. Take turns with other band members.*

The **BREATH MARK** tells you to take a deep breath through your mouth.

A BREATH OF FRESH AIR—*Name each note before you play.*

BREATHING EASY—*Sing the notes, then play.*

THREE-ZY DOES IT!—*Practice playing three different notes in a row.*

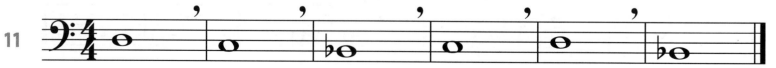

HALF NOTES receive two beats (counts) in 4/4 time.

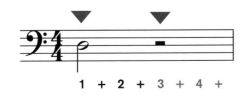

1 + 2 + 3 + 4 +

HALF RESTS receive two beats (counts) of silence and look similar to whole rests. Since half rests only contain two beats, they are "light" and therefore float above the line. Because most whole rests contain an entire measure of beats, they are "heavier" and therefore sink below the line.

The **REPEAT SIGN** tells you to go back to the beginning and play the piece again.

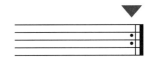

HALF THE TIME—*Introducing half notes and half rests. Repeat as indicated. Clap the rhythm as you count the beats, then sing the piece before you play.*

12

1 + 2 + 3 + 4 +   1 + 2 + 3 + 4 +

MIX IT UP—*Play each group of half notes in one breath while changing notes.*

13

A **DUET** is a composition for two performers. When both parts are played together, you will sometimes hear two different notes played at the same time which creates **HARMONY**.

14   **DUET? DO IT!**—*Introducing our first duet.*

A

B

NAME THE NOTES—*Write the name of each note in the space provided, then sing the notes before you play.*

15

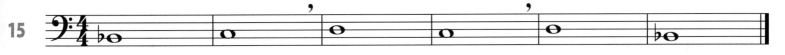

___   ___   ___   ___   ___   ___

QUARTER NOTES receive one beat (count) in 4/4 time.
QUARTER RESTS receive one beat (count) of silence.

1 + 2 + 3 + 4 +   1 + 2 + 3 + 4 +

QUARTER NOTES—*Introducing quarter notes and quarter rests. Play each group of notes in one breath. Count, clap and sing before you play.*

16

1 + 2 + 3 + 4 +   1 + 2 + 3 + 4 +

QUARTERLY REPORT—*Name each note before you play.*

17

A **PHRASE** is a musical idea that ends with a breath.

HOT CROSS BUNS—*Play the phrase, not just the notes!*

English Folk Song

18

OUR FOURTH NOTE *Introducing the new note, E♭.*

19

SCALING THE WALL—*Practice using your newest note. Breathe only at the breath marks and rests.*

20

OUR FIFTH NOTE *Introducing the new note, F.*

21

SCALING NEW HEIGHTS—*Practice using another new note.*

22

MERRILY WE ROLL ALONG—*Breath marks help define the phrases.*

Traditional

AU CLAIRE DE LA LUNE—*More phrase and note practice. Add breath marks to create your own musical phrases.*

French Folk Song

COMMON TIME is another name for the $\frac{4}{4}$ time signature and is indicated with this symbol:

A **FERMATA** tells you to hold a note or rest longer than its normal duration.

A **COMPOSER** is a person who writes music. Look for the composer's name on the upper right corner of the music.

Who wrote the music to *Jingle Bells*?

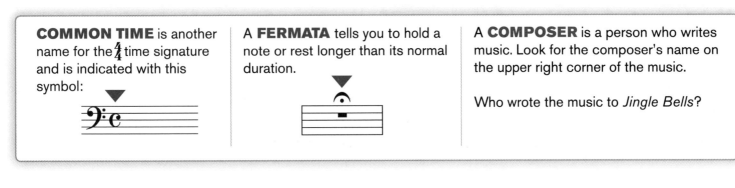

JINGLE BELLS—*Play this piece in common time and notice the fermata at the end. Count, clap and sing before you play.*

James Lord Pierpont

1 + 2 + 3 + 4 +

GO TELL AUNT RHODY—*More practice in common time with a fermata.*

American Folk Song

LIGHTLY ROW—*Play this duet in common time. Switch parts on the repeat.*

Traditional

A

B

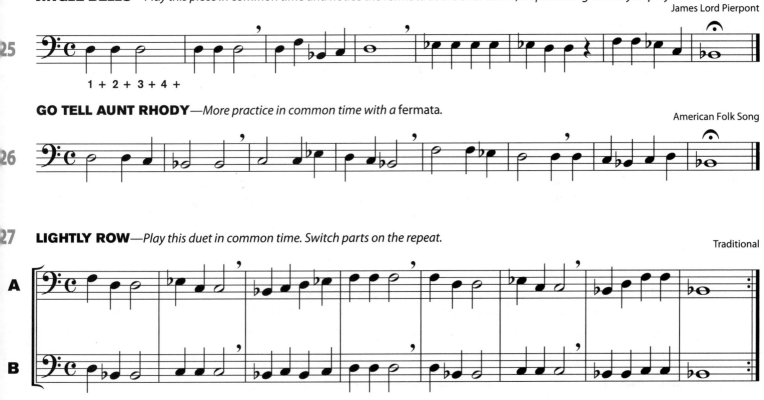

TUTTI tells you that everyone plays together.

GOOD KING WENCESLAS—*The soloist and full band take turns playing.*

Traditional English Carol

solo   tutti   solo   tutti

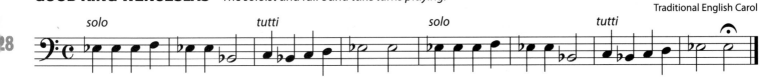

A **ROUND** is a type of music in which players start the piece at different times, creating interesting harmonies and accompaniments.

SWEETLY SINGS THE DONKEY (round)—*Play this round by having players or groups start every four measures. This piece continues on the next staff, which does not need to show the meter.*

American Folk Song

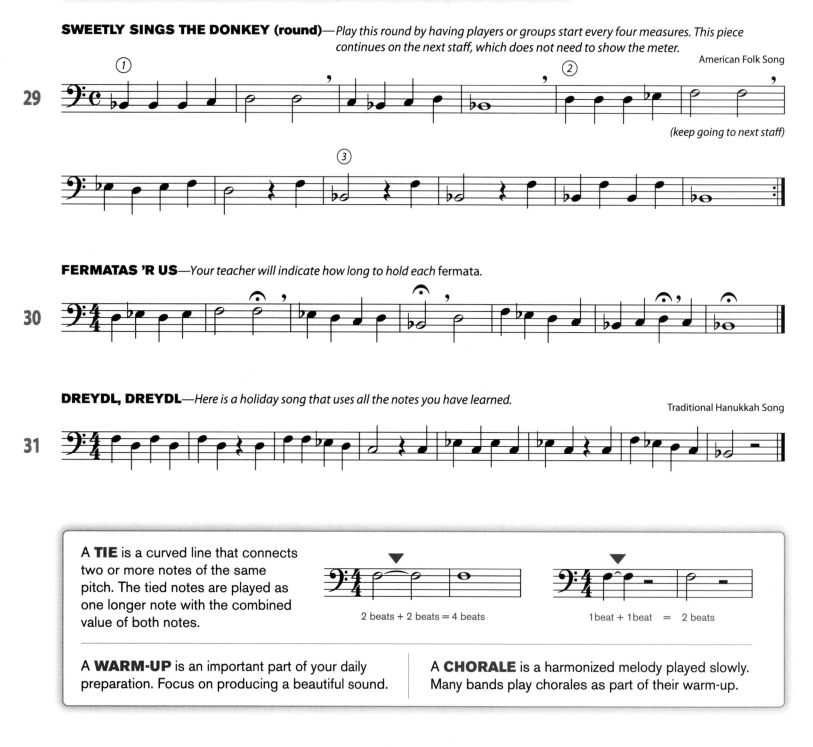

(keep going to next staff)

FERMATAS 'R US—*Your teacher will indicate how long to hold each fermata.*

DREYDL, DREYDL—*Here is a holiday song that uses all the notes you have learned.*

Traditional Hanukkah Song

A **TIE** is a curved line that connects two or more notes of the same pitch. The tied notes are played as one longer note with the combined value of both notes.

2 beats + 2 beats = 4 beats   1 beat + 1 beat = 2 beats

A **WARM-UP** is an important part of your daily preparation. Focus on producing a beautiful sound.

A **CHORALE** is a harmonized melody played slowly. Many bands play chorales as part of their warm-up.

WARM-UP CHORALE—*Play with a beautiful sustained tone. Listen for the harmony!*

TIE AND TIE AGAIN—*Play the tied notes full value. This piece can be played as a duet along with the Warm-Up Chorale.*

▶ Complete the **SOUND CHECK** near the end of your book.

Level 2: Sound Fundamentals

OUR SIXTH NOTE *Introducing the new note, G.*

34 **G**

TWINKLING STARS—*Play this familiar melody using your new note.*

Adapted by Wolfgang Amadeus Mozart

35

(keep going to next staff)

36 **JOLLY OLD ST. NICK**—*Here is a duet that uses your new note.*

Traditional Carol

A

B

New Time Signature (Meter) 2/4 TIME

2 = Two beats (counts) per measure.
4 = A quarter note receives one beat (count).

RHYTHMS IN 2/4—*Clap the rhythm while counting the beats aloud.*

1 + 2 + 1 + 2 + 1 + 2 + 1 + 2 +

TWO-FOUR OUT THE DOOR—*This exercise has two beats per measure. Count, clap and sing before you play.*

37

1 + 2 + 1 + 2 +

LONDON BRIDGE—*Here's a melody you know in 2/4 time. How many beats does the last note receive?*

English Folk Song

38

TWO-FOUR OLD MAC—*Name each note before you play.*

Traditional

39

12

TECHNIQUE BUILDER—*Practice slowly at first, then gradually get faster each time you play.*

40

SOUNDS NEW! *Introducing the new note, low A.*

41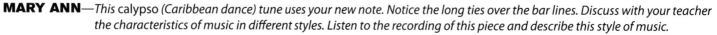

MARY ANN—*This calypso (Caribbean dance) tune uses your new note. Notice the long ties over the bar lines. Discuss with your teacher the characteristics of music in different styles. Listen to the recording of this piece and describe this style of music.*

Caribbean Folk Song

42

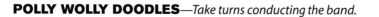

CONDUCTORS lead groups of musicians using specific hand and arm patterns.

Conduct the **2/4** pattern with your right hand.

2
1
(conductor's view)

REHEARSAL MARKS are reference numbers or letters in a box above the staff. They are also called *rehearsal numbers* or *letters*. They help musicians find logical places to start and stop when learning the piece.

▼
9

POLLY WOLLY DOODLES—*Take turns conducting the band.*

American Folk Song

43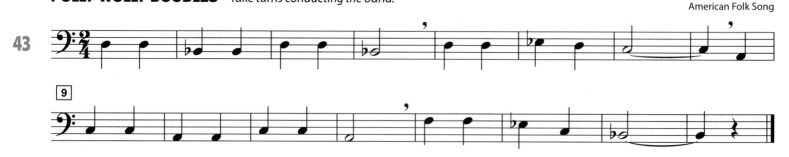

9

44 **DUET OF THE CRUSADERS**—*This duet uses your new high and low notes.*

German Folk Song

SHOO-FLY!—*This melody features ties across the bar line.*

American Folk Song

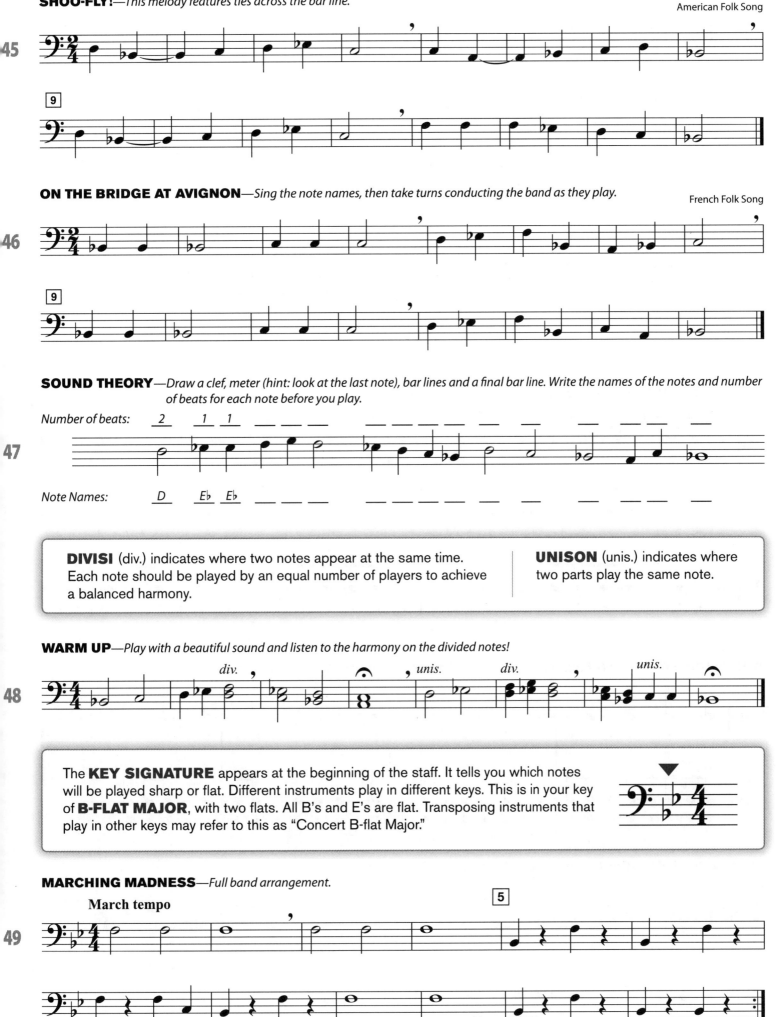

ON THE BRIDGE AT AVIGNON—*Sing the note names, then take turns conducting the band as they play.*

French Folk Song

SOUND THEORY—*Draw a clef, meter (hint: look at the last note), bar lines and a final bar line. Write the names of the notes and number of beats for each note before you play.*

Number of beats: 2   1   1

Note Names: D   E♭   E♭

DIVISI (div.) indicates where two notes appear at the same time. Each note should be played by an equal number of players to achieve a balanced harmony.

UNISON (unis.) indicates where two parts play the same note.

WARM UP—*Play with a beautiful sound and listen to the harmony on the divided notes!*

The **KEY SIGNATURE** appears at the beginning of the staff. It tells you which notes will be played sharp or flat. Different instruments play in different keys. This is in your key of **B-FLAT MAJOR**, with two flats. All B's and E's are flat. Transposing instruments that play in other keys may refer to this as "Concert B-flat Major."

MARCHING MADNESS—*Full band arrangement.*

March tempo

ROCK THIS BAND!—*Full band arrangement.*

Hard rock

EIGHTH NOTES each receive a half beat (count) in 4/4 time. Two eighth notes receive one count. Eighth notes often appear in pairs or in groups of four and have a *beam* across the note stems.

RHYTHM ROUND-UP—*Clap the rhythm as you count the beats.*

GOTTA HAND IT TO YA! (Clapping Duet)—*Clap either Part A or B, then switch parts on the repeat.*

PIECES OF EIGHT—*Count the rhythm first, clap, then play.*

DYNAMICS in music refer to the change in volume you create when playing loud or soft. Italian terms are often used in music. The term we use for loud is **FORTE** and is indicated by the letter f, and the term we use for quiet (or soft) is **PIANO** and is indicated by the letter p.

WHISPER AND SHOUT!—*Play the notes with the dynamics indicated.*

(look ahead to the next line for the dynamic change)

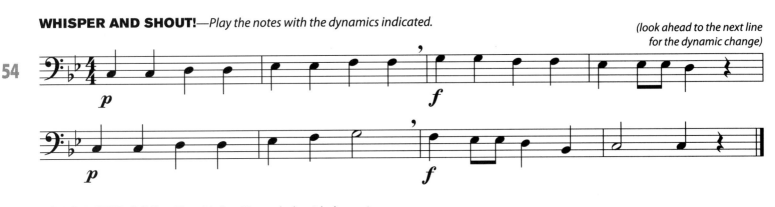

LONG, LONG AGO—*Play this familiar melody with dynamics.*

Thomas Haynes Bayly

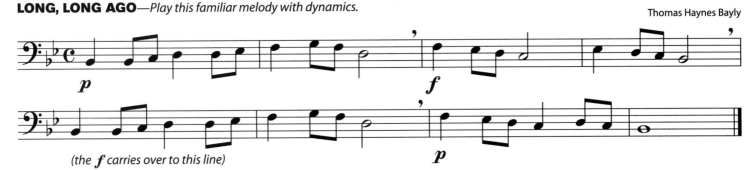

(the f carries over to this line)

SKIP TO MY LOU—*More fun with dynamics! Name each note before you play.*

American Folk Song

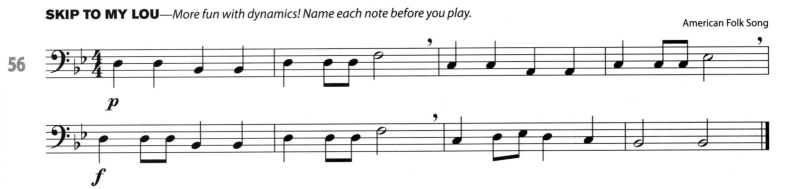

57 **DYNAMIC DUET**—*Read the dynamics carefully as they are different in each part. Switch parts on the repeat.*

THIS OLD MAN—*Here is a tune to play just for fun!*

An **INTERVAL** is the distance between two notes. The interval of an 8th is called an **OCTAVE**. The interval on the same note is a **UNISON**.

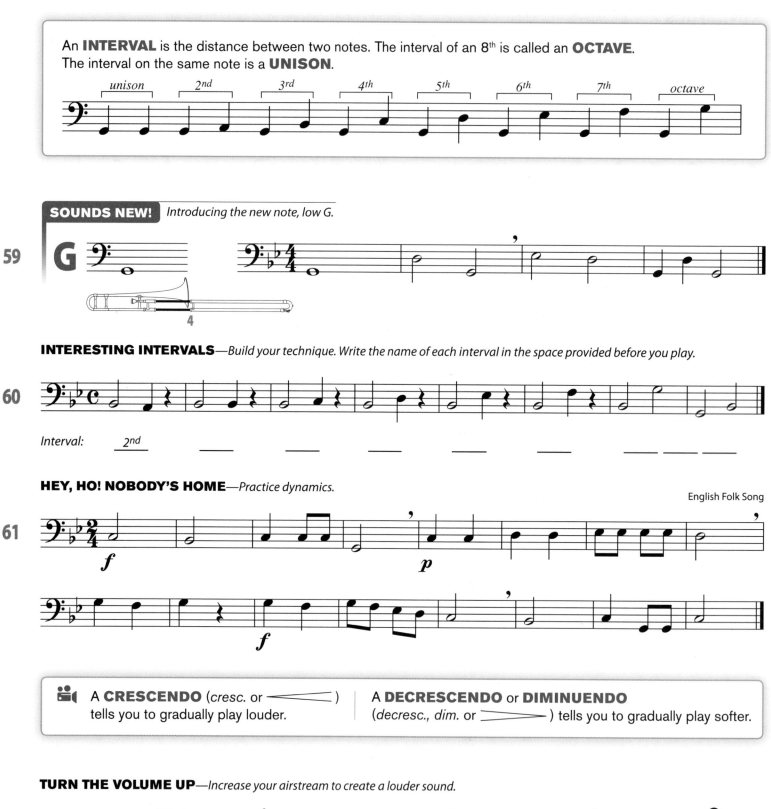

SOUNDS NEW! *Introducing the new note, low G.*

59 G

INTERESTING INTERVALS—*Build your technique. Write the name of each interval in the space provided before you play.*

60

Interval: _____2nd_____ _____ _____ _____ _____ _____ _____ _____

HEY, HO! NOBODY'S HOME—*Practice dynamics.*

English Folk Song

61

A **CRESCENDO** (*cresc.* or ⟨) tells you to gradually play louder. | A **DECRESCENDO** or **DIMINUENDO** (*decresc.*, *dim.* or ⟩) tells you to gradually play softer.

TURN THE VOLUME UP—*Increase your airstream to create a louder sound.*

62

TURN THE VOLUME DOWN—*Reduce your airstream to create a softer sound. For extra fun, play this with* Turn the Volume Up *as a duet.*

63

17

A **SLUR** is a curved line connecting two or more notes. Begin the first note of a slur with a regular "tah" or "toe" tonguing style. Trombone slurs require a quick slide movement between notes and the use of a very light tongue (du or dah) on the other notes under the slur to avoid a smear from one note to the next.

▶ *Slurring & Glissando*

tongue   tongue   tongue   slur   tongue tongue tongue   tongue   slur   slur

FRÈRE JACQUES (round)—*Practice the slurs in this familiar melody, then play it as a round.*

French Folk Song

64

f

p

PICKUP NOTES occur before the first complete measure of a phrase. Often the last measure of the piece will be missing the same number of beats as the pickup notes have.

4 +   1 + 2 + 3 + 4 +   1 + 2 + 3 +

A TISKET, A TASKET—*How many beats are in the pickup?*

American Folk Song

65

f
4 + 1 + 2 + 3 + 4 +

decresc.

p   *cresc.*   *f*

1 + 2 + 3 +
(beat 4 is the pickup)

JASMINE FLOWER—*Practice the notes and skills you have learned.*

Chinese Folk Song

66

p

f

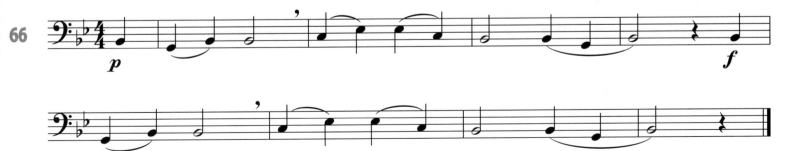

ERIE CANAL—*How many beats are in the pickup? How many beats are missing from the last measure?*

Thomas S. Allen

67

OH! SUSANNAH—*The pickup contains two eighth notes.*

Stephen Foster

68

THEME AND VARIATION is a compositional technique in which the composer clearly states a melody (or theme), then changes it by adding contrasting variations.

A **DOUBLE BAR LINE** indicates the end of a section.

THEME AND VARIATIONS ON BLACK SHEEP—*How does* Variation I *differ from the* Theme? *How does* Variation II *differ from the* Theme?

English Folk Song

69

Theme

Variation I

Variation II

THEME AND VARIATIONS YOUR WAY—*Write your own variation by changing the rhythm and/or notes, then play it!*

Theme: *Hot Cross Buns*

70

Variation: *Cinnamon Buns*

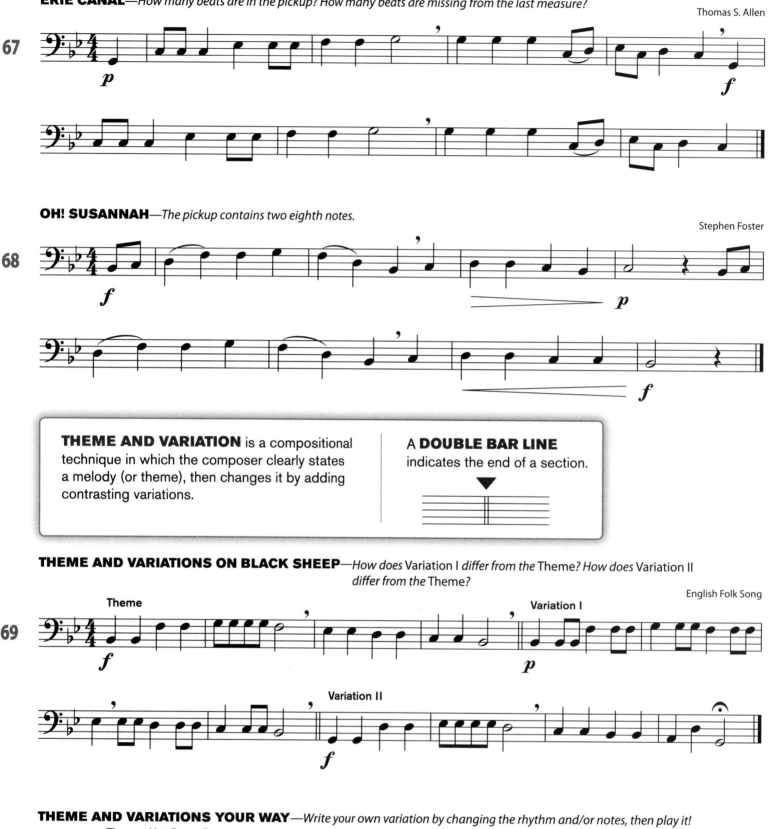

TEMPO MARKINGS indicate the speed of the music.

LARGO is a slow tempo.
ANDANTE is a moderate walking tempo.
ALLEGRO is a fast tempo.

Conduct the $\frac{4}{4}$ pattern with your right hand.

Conduct each piece below at the correct tempo.

(conductor's view)

Austrian composer **Wolfgang Amadeus Mozart** (1756–1791) was one of the most influential musicians of the Classical period. Though he only lived to the age of 35, he was very prolific and is known for his symphonies, operas, chamber music and piano pieces.

German-born composer **Johannes Brahms** (1833–1897) was one of the leading figures of the Romantic period in music history. Brahms is best known for his four symphonies, two piano concertos and his remarkable choral work *A German Requiem*.

SERENADE—*Full band arrangement.*

Wolfgang Amadeus Mozart

INVADERS!—*Full band arrangement. Remember, in $\frac{2}{4}$ time a whole measure rest receives two beats.*

ACADEMIC FESTIVAL OVERTURE—*Full band arrangement.*

Johannes Brahms

STODOLA PUMPA—*Practice good posture and breathing skills.*

Czech Folk Song

More dynamics! **MEZZO FORTE** (*mf*) is medium loud. **MEZZO PIANO** (*mp*) is medium soft.

DYNAMITE DYNAMICS—*Review all four of the dynamics you've learned, along with* crescendo *and* decrescendo.

Stephen Collins Foster (1826–1864), best known for composing songs such as *Beautiful Dreamer*, *Oh! Susanna* and *Camptown Races*, is often called "the father of American music" and the "first professional songwriter."

MY OLD KENTUCKY HOME—*Solo with piano accompaniment.*

Piano Accompaniment

▶ Complete the **SOUND CHECK** near the end of your book.

Level 3: Sound Musicianship

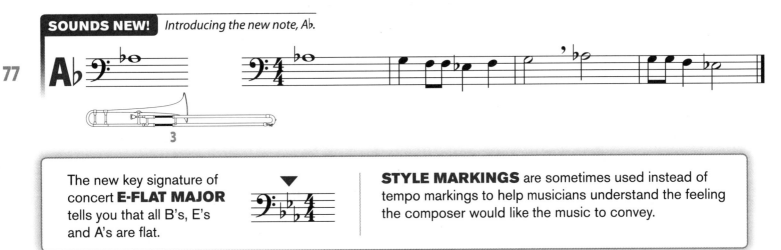

SOUNDS NEW! *Introducing the new note, A♭.*

77

The new key signature of concert **E-FLAT MAJOR** tells you that all B's, E's and A's are flat.

STYLE MARKINGS are sometimes used instead of tempo markings to help musicians understand the feeling the composer would like the music to convey.

WAY UP HIGH—*Before you play, circle all the notes affected by the key signature. Discuss ways in which you can make this sound "sweet."*

Sweetly

78

mf

BINGO—*Before playing, discuss ways in which you can make this sound "light." Name the key.*

American Folk Song

Lightly

79

mp

f

1ST AND 2ND ENDINGS: Play the 1st ending the first time through. Repeat the music, but skip over the 1st ending on the repeat and play the 2nd ending instead.

1st Time _____ | 1. | 2.

2nd Time _____

BUFFALO GALS—*Since this is played with spirit, the tempo should be energetic! Watch the 1st and 2nd endings.*

American Traditional

With spirit!

80

mf

1.

f

2.

f

MUSETTE—*Here is a tune to play just for fun!*

Johann Sebastian Bach

Andante

81

mf

mp

1.

2.

¾ TIME is a meter in which there are 3 beats per measure and the quarter note receives 1 beat.

1 + 2 + 3 +   1 + 2 + 3 +   1 + 2 + 3 +   1 + 2 + 3 +

MEXICAN HAT DANCE—*Write the number of each beat you play in the space provided. Count, clap and sing before you play.*
See how well your performance of Mexican Hat Dance *captures the style of a dance.*

Mexican Folk Song

Allegro

82

mf 1 2 3

1.   2.

A **DOT** increases the length of a note by half its value. Since a half note receives 2 counts, the dot that follows receives 1 count. Therefore, a **DOTTED HALF NOTE** receives 3 beats in both ¾ and 4/4 time.

1 + 2 + 3 +   1 + 2 + 3 +   1 + 2 + 3 +   1 + 2 + 3 +

BARCAROLLE—*Name the key. Look for the breath marks to help you phrase and play this in a gentle style.*
Try memorizing this melody and playing it expressively.

Jacques Offenbach

Gently

83

1 + 2 + 3 +
mp

Conduct the ¾ pattern with your right hand.

1 2 3
(conductor's view)

Edvard Grieg (1843–1907) was a Norwegian composer and pianist of the Romantic period. He is best known for his *Piano Concerto in A minor* and his wonderful *Peer Gynt Suite*, which includes the famous *In the Hall of the Mountain King* and *Morning*.

MORNING—*Before you play, sing and conduct the following piece.* Moderato *is a medium tempo.*

Edvard Grieg

Moderato

84

mf

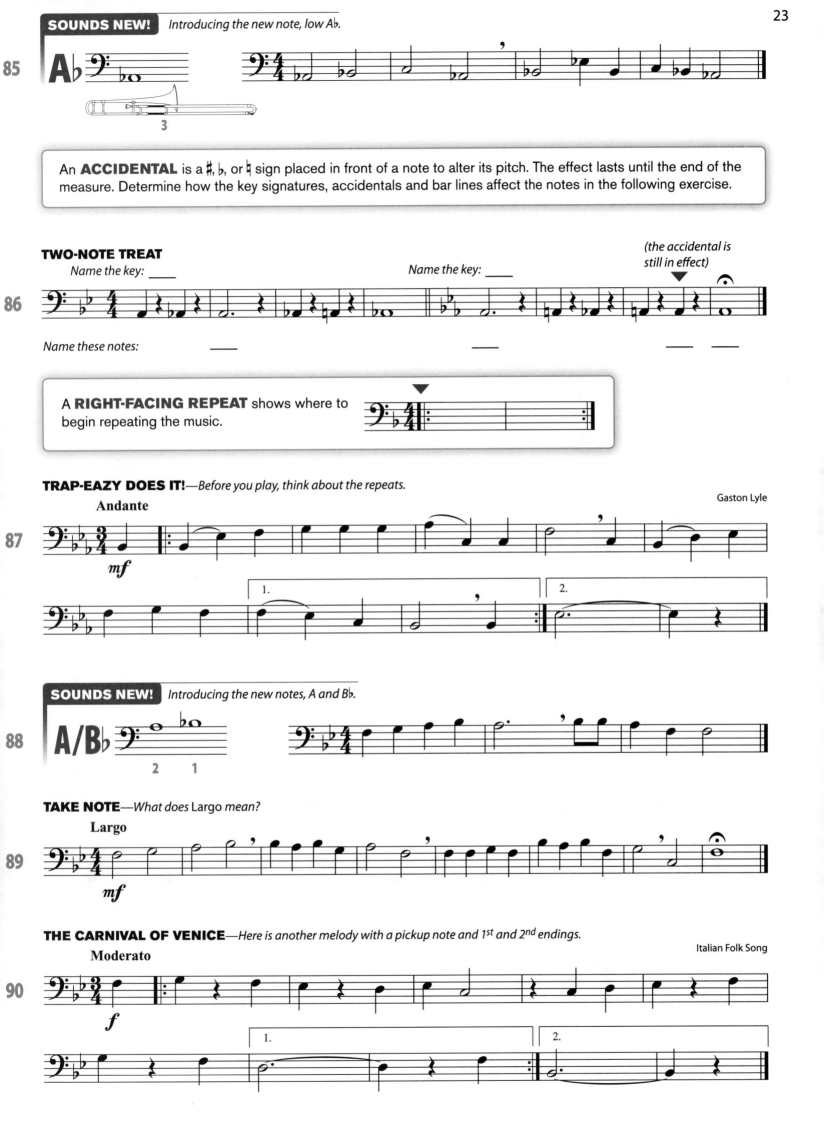

SOUNDS NEW! *Introducing the new note, low A♭.*

85

An **ACCIDENTAL** is a ♯, ♭, or ♮ sign placed in front of a note to alter its pitch. The effect lasts until the end of the measure. Determine how the key signatures, accidentals and bar lines affect the notes in the following exercise.

TWO-NOTE TREAT

Name the key: ____   *Name the key:* ____

(the accidental is still in effect)

86

Name these notes: ____   ____   ____ ____

A **RIGHT-FACING REPEAT** shows where to begin repeating the music.

TRAP-EAZY DOES IT!—*Before you play, think about the repeats.*

Gaston Lyle

Andante

87

mf

1.   2.

SOUNDS NEW! *Introducing the new notes, A and B♭.*

A/B♭

88

2   1

TAKE NOTE—*What does Largo mean?*

Largo

89

mf

THE CARNIVAL OF VENICE—*Here is another melody with a pickup note and 1ˢᵗ and 2ⁿᵈ endings.*

Italian Folk Song

Moderato

90

f

1.   2.

An **ARTICULATION** indicates the way a note should be played. An **ACCENT** is an articulation that tells you the note should be played with a stronger attack.

CHESTER—Chester *was often referred to as the "unofficial anthem" of the American Revolution.*

William Billings

Proudly

A **ONE-MEASURE REPEAT** means to play the previous measure again.

EIGHTH NOTES and **EIGHTH RESTS** are not always in pairs. They can be single notes and rests. Single eighth notes have a flag on the stem rather than a beam.

MARCHING ALONG—*Circle the accents and the one-measure repeat before you play.*

Moderate march tempo

93 EXERCISES ON EIGHTHS—*Demonstrate your understanding of eighth notes and rests by clapping these exercises. Switch parts on the repeat.*

94 EMPHASIS ON ACCENTS—*Try both parts of this clapping duet and be sure to clap louder on the accented notes. Before you play, circle the single eighth notes and eighth rests in Part B.*

EMPHASIS ON NOTES—*Now play the accents by using more air to make the accented notes louder.*

Andante

DOWN BY THE STATION—*Practice eighth notes, slurs and accents.*

American Folk Song

96

BROTHER JOHN (round)—*More practice using articulations (slurs and accents) and one-measure repeats, then play it as a round.*

French Folk Song

97

SOUNDS NEW! *Introducing the new note, E.*

98

The new key signature of concert **F MAJOR** tells you that all B's are flat.

BREATHING: Breath marks have been included so far to show you where to breathe. Now you can determine this yourself by finding logical places to take a breath, such as during rests and at the end of a phrase.

AURA LEE—*How does this new key signature affect the notes you will play?*

George R. Poulton

99

SAKURA—*This melody has a right-facing repeat. Before you play, trace your finger over the "roadmap" of the piece.*

Japanese Folk Song

100

SHE WORE A YELLOW RIBBON—*Here's a tune to play just for fun!*

George A. Norton

101

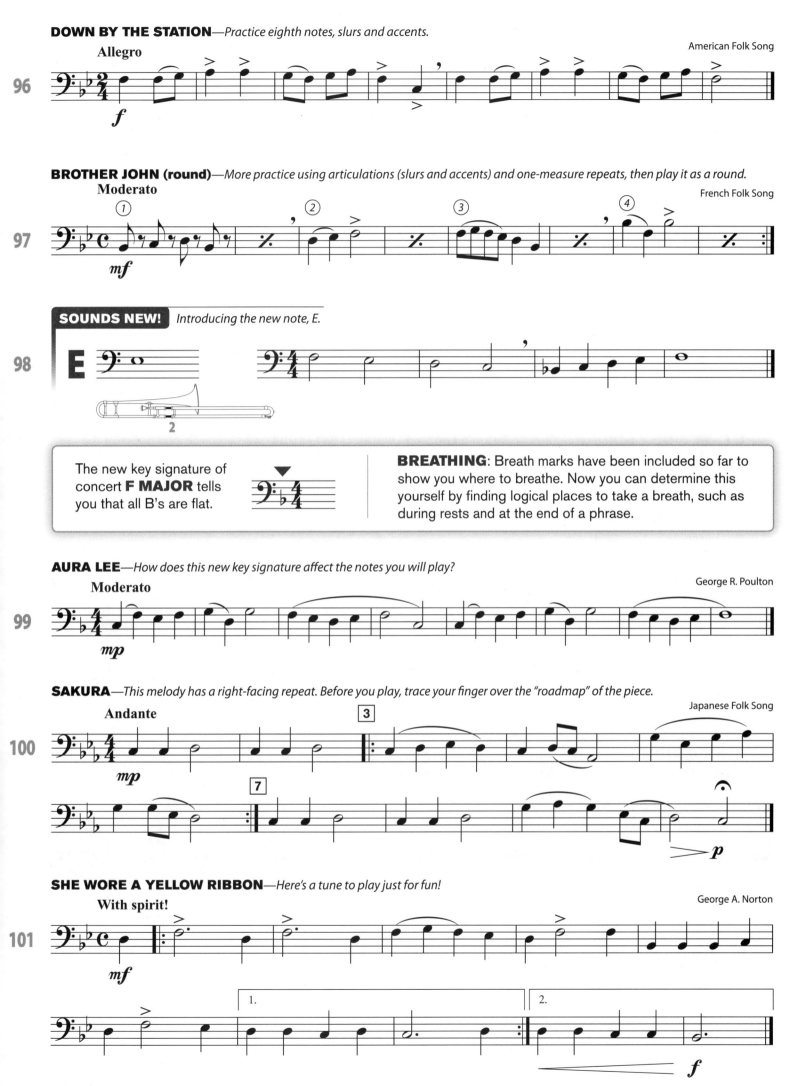

A quarter note receives 1 beat, and the dot that follows receives ½ a beat, therefore, a **DOTTED QUARTER NOTE** receives 1½ beats and can be subdivided into three eighth notes. (♩. = ♪♪♪)

Count and clap, then play this rhythm. Notice that the quarter note tied to the eighth sounds the same as the dotted quarter note.

A WHOLE LOTTA TIES—*Feel the pulse of the beat on the tied eighth note.*

Moderato

102

A WHOLE LOTTA DOTS—*Feel the pulse of the beat on the dot.*

Moderato

103

D.C. AL FINE indicates to repeat from the beginning and play to the **FINE** (the end).

Antonín Leopold Dvořák (1841–1904) was a Czech composer of the Romantic period best known for drawing inspiration from folk music and for his remarkable *New World Symphony* and *Slavonic Dances*.

THEME FROM THE "NEW WORLD SYMPHONY"—*Play the D.C., then end at the* Fine.

Antonín Dvořák

Largo

104

▶ *Fine*

▶ *D.C. al Fine*

SYNCOPATION occurs when there is emphasis on a weak beat.

JOY TO THE WORLD—*Full band arrangement.*

Christmas Carol

Joyfully

105

9

17 (syncopation)

COURTESY ACCIDENTALS help remind you of the key signature. They usually occur after another accidental or a recent key change. These special accidentals are enclosed in parentheses.

ACCIDENTAL ENCOUNTERS—*Before you play, name all the notes.*

(notice the key signature change)

D.S. AL FINE indicates to repeat from the sign (𝄋) and play to the *Fine*.

German composer **Ludwig van Beethoven** (1770–1827), despite losing his hearing, composed a vast number of works including string quartets and concertos. He is best known for his nine symphonies, especially his renowned *Fifth Symphony*.

ODE TO JOY—*Maestoso means to play majestically. Circle the "sign" then clap, count and sing before you play.*

Ludwig van Beethoven

A **MULTIPLE-MEASURE REST** tells you to rest for more than one full measure. The number above the staff tells you how many measures you rest.

AULD LANG SYNE—*Full band arrangement. Circle the multiple-measure rest before you play.*

Scottish Folk Song

MICHAEL, ROW THE BOAT ASHORE—*Always play with a beautiful sound.*

African-American Spiritual

▶ Complete the **SOUND CHECK** near the end of your book.

Level 4: Sound Development

A **SCALE** is a series of notes that ascend or descend stepwise (consecutive notes) within a key. The lowest and the highest notes of the scale are always the same letter name and are an octave apart.

A **WALTZ** is a popular dance in ¾ time.

CONCERT B♭ MAJOR SCALE—*Memorize this scale!*

110

THREE-FOUR, PHRASE SOME MORE—*This melody starts with a phrase that sounds as if it asks a question, followed by a phrase that sounds as if it provides the answer. Play this as a duet with the Concert B♭ scale.*

Waltz tempo

111

DOWN THE ROAD—*Play with a steady stream of fast air.*

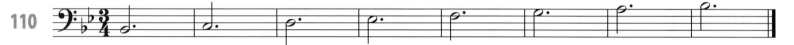

112

SUO GAN—*Play this melody in the style of a lullaby.*

Moderato

Welsh Folk Song

113

LEGATO (–) is an articulation or style of playing that is smooth and connected. It is indicated by a line.

STACCATO (·) is an articulation or style of playing that is light and separated. It is indicated with a dot.

ARTICULATION STATION—*Play the notes with the indicated articulation.* ▶ *Articulation Station: Accents, Staccato, and Legato*

114

OVERTURE TO "WILLIAM TELL"—*Here is a familiar tune that uses* legato *and* staccato.

Allegro

Gioacchino Rossini

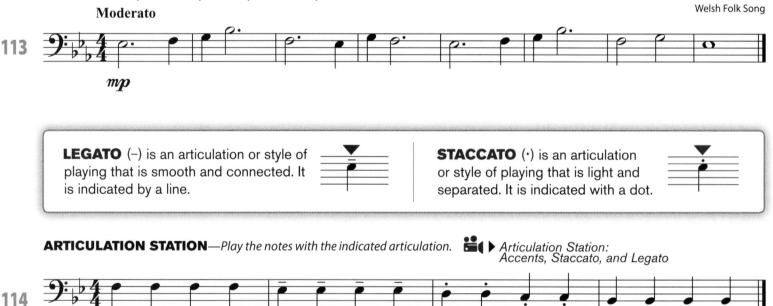

115

SOUNDS NEW! *Introducing the new note, D♭.*

116

ALGERIAN DANCE—*Try out your new note on this exotic melody.*

Arabic Folk Song

Andante

117

mf

THE LONG AND SHORT, COMMON TIME, ACCIDENTAL BLUES—*Try out your new articulation skills! The blues is a type of American music derived from spirituals and work songs.*

Medium blues tempo

118

f

The new key signature of concert **A-FLAT MAJOR** tells you that all B's, E's, A's and D's are flat.

ON TOP OF OLD SMOKEY—*Before you play, look at your key signature and circle all the notes that will be affected. Notice the length of the tied notes.*

American Folk Song

Moderately

119

f

LONG AND SHORT ACCIDENTAL ENCOUNTERS—*Before you play, name all the notes. Watch out for the key change! Try this as a duet with* The Long and Short, Common Time, Accidental Blues.

Medium blues tempo

120

mf

GOOD NIGHT LADIES—*Demonstrate good posture and breathing skills.*

Traditional

Brightly

121

mf   *f*

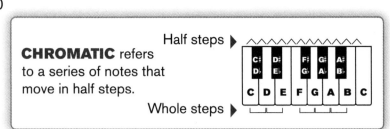

CHROMATIC refers to a series of notes that move in half steps.

CHROMATIC MARCH—Alla marcia *instructs us to play in the style of a march.*

Alla marcia

122

123 **JAZZ DOO-ETTE**—*Play this piece in the style of the "jazz big bands" popular in the 1930s and 1940s. Name the key.*

Swing

ON YOUR OWN!—*Play the first four measures, then write the last four measures yourself! Now, play the entire piece.*

Andante

124

MUSIC MY WAY! Write your own composition:
- Write in the clef, meter, key signature, tempo and style you choose.
- Place the notes and rhythms that you already know on the staff in any order you like and add a final bar line.
- Add articulations (staccato, legato, accents, slurs) and dynamics (*p*, *mp*, *mf*, *f*, cresc., decresc.).
- Give the piece a title, and be sure to add **YOUR NAME** as the composer.
- Now play the piece for your friends and family!

Title: _____   *Composed by* _____

CAN-CAN—*Vivo means lively and spirited!*

Jacques Offenbach

Vivo

125

VOLGA BOAT SONG—Pesante *means to play in a heavy style. Memorize this piece and play in an expressive manner.*

Russian Folk Song

With your teacher, develop a list of rules for good concert etiquette. Some things to include might be to listen quietly and to show your appreciation by applauding at the end of the piece. Take turns performing *All Through the Night* while others in your class practice good concert etiquette.

ALL THROUGH THE NIGHT—*Name the key.*

Welsh Folk Song

ARIRANG—*Name the key. Discuss with your teacher the characteristics of music from different cultures. Listen to the recording of this piece and describe those characteristics.*

Korean Folk Song

MINUET—*A minuet is a French country dance.*

Johann Sebastian Bach

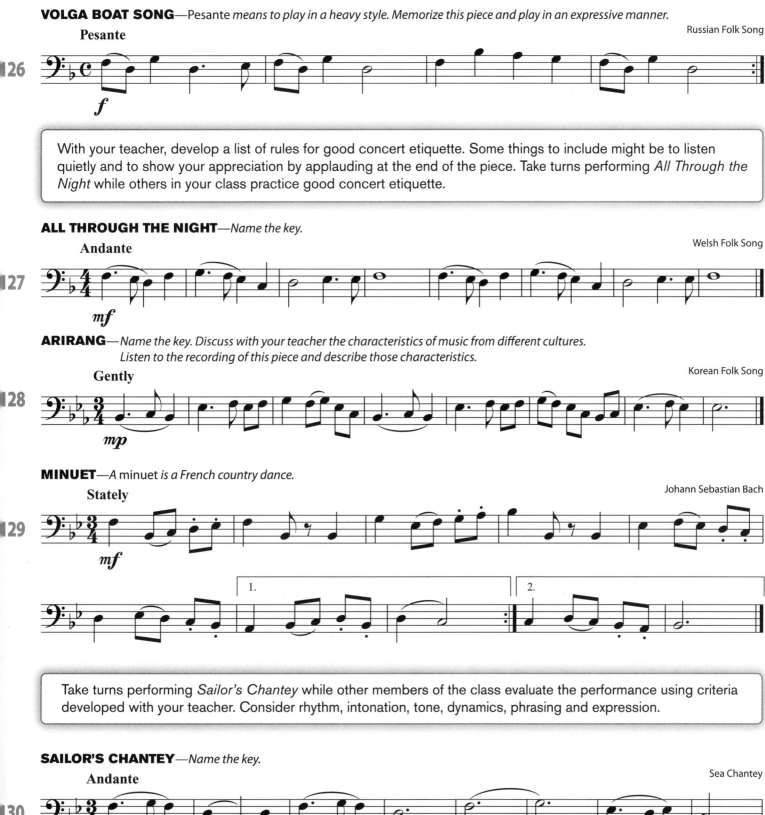

Take turns performing *Sailor's Chantey* while other members of the class evaluate the performance using criteria developed with your teacher. Consider rhythm, intonation, tone, dynamics, phrasing and expression.

SAILOR'S CHANTEY—*Name the key.*

Sea Chantey

THEME FROM SWAN LAKE—*Always play with expression.*

Pyotr Il'yich Tchaikovsky

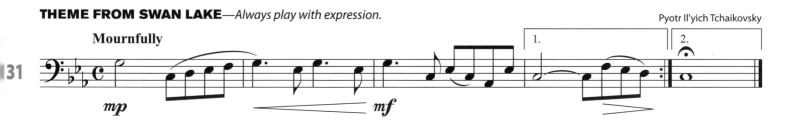

Most of the music we hear is either in a **MAJOR** key or a **MINOR** key. The sound of these keys is created by the arrangement of half steps and whole steps. The mood of a major key is often cheerful or heroic, while a minor key may be sad or solemn.

MAJOR MACARONI (YANKEE DOODLE)—*This is in a major key. How does this make you feel?*

American Traditional

MINOR MACARONI—*This is in a minor key. How does this make you feel? How is it different from Major Macaroni?*

ALOUETTE—*Is this in a major or minor key?*

French-Canadian Folk Song

HATIKVAH—*Does this sound like a major or minor key?*

Israeli National Anthem

MARCH SLAV—*Is this in a major or minor key?*

Pyotr Il'yich Tchaikovsky

▶ Complete the **SOUND CHECK** near the end of your book.

Level 5: Sound Techniques

LIP SLURS are played by keeping the embouchure firm and the airstream supported while slurring two notes that have the same fingering.

An **INTERLUDE** is a short musical piece. The following *Imperative Interludes* will help you practice lip slurs when playing large intervals.

RANGE ROVER 1

137

IMPERATIVE INTERLUDE 1

138

RANGE ROVER 2

139

IMPERATIVE INTERLUDE 2

140

RANGE ROVER 3—A **GLISSANDO** *(Gliss.) is played by moving your slide slowly between the two notes while maintaining a steady stream of air.*

NEW SLIDE POSITION *Introducing the alternate slide position for F.*

F 6th position

141

IMPERATIVE INTERLUDE 3

142

HIGH FLYING—*Here's a tune to play just for fun!*

Andante

143

mf

RANGE ROVER 4—*Use 6th position F when moving to low C.*

144

IMPERATIVE INTERLUDE 4—*Use 6th position F when moving to or from low C.*

145

RANGE ROVER 5

146

IMPERATIVE INTERLUDE 5

147

RANGE ROVER 6

148

IMPERATIVE INTERLUDE 6

149

DRINK TO ME ONLY WITH THINE EYES—*Practice your slurs with this familiar tune.*

Moderato

Traditional English Song

150

mf

IT'S RAINING, IT'S POURING—*Play this familiar melody with a beautiful sound.*

English Folk Song

IT'S WINDY, IT'S STORMING—*Try playing this piece as a duet with* It's Raining, It's Pouring.

RANGE RIDER

CRAZY FINGERS

RANGE ROVER 7

IMPERATIVE INTERLUDE 7

SWORD DANCE—*Here's a tune to play just for fun!*

Traditional

BREAK UP—*Play the phrase, not just the notes.*

NEW NOTE! *Introducing the new note, high C.*

158

3rd position

BREAK DOWN—*Play with a steady stream of fast air.*

159

DOWN AND OUT—*Play with a full sound.*

Moderato

160

mf

UP AND OVER—*Demonstrate good posture.*

Moderato

161

mf

THE CONCERT B♭ MAJOR SCALE—*Memorize the following ascending and descending scale.*

162

An **ARPEGGIO** is the 1st, 3rd, 5th and 8th notes of the scale.

COUNTRY GARDENS—*Name the key. Before you play, notice how loud the crescendo becomes.*

Allegro

English Folk Song

163

mp   *f*

CAMPTOWN RACES—*Before you play, notice how soft or loud each dynamic change becomes.*

Lively

Stephen Foster

164

f   *dim.*   *mf*   *cresc.*   *f*

decresc.   *p*   *f*

WHEN THE SAINTS GO MARCHING IN—*Full band arrangement.*

American Gospel Hymn

165

Austrian composer **Franz Joseph Haydn** (1732–1809) was one of the most important composers of the Classical period. He is best known for his many symphonies, string quartets, masses, and his oratorios *The Creation* and *The Seasons.*

SURPRISE SYMPHONY—*This piece includes a "surprise" created by dynamics. Can you find the big surprise? Discuss with your teacher the characteristics of music written during this period. Listen to the recording of this piece and describe those characteristics.*

Franz Joseph Haydn

166

HALF-STEP HASSLE—*Practice your chromatic skills.*

167

HILARIOUS HALF STEPS—*Here is another chromatic challenge. Name the notes before you play.*

168

SYMPHONIC THEME FROM SYMPHONY NO. 1—*Is this a major or minor key?*

Gustav Mahler

169

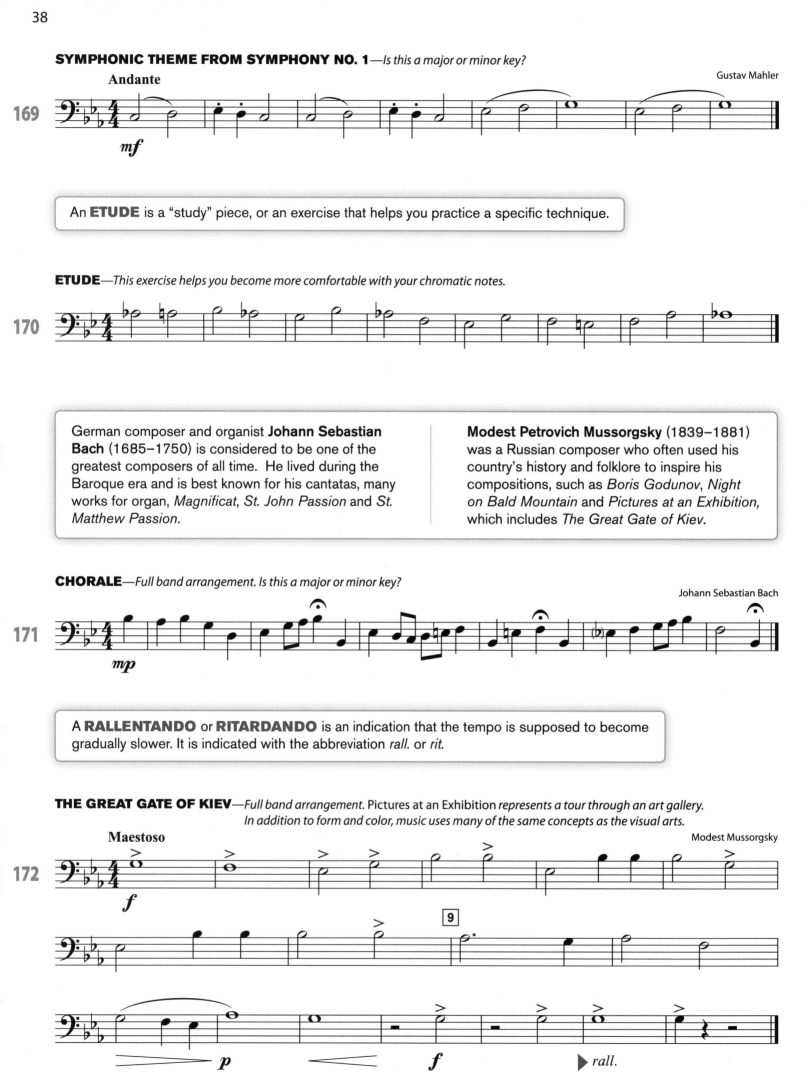

An **ETUDE** is a "study" piece, or an exercise that helps you practice a specific technique.

ETUDE—*This exercise helps you become more comfortable with your chromatic notes.*

170

German composer and organist **Johann Sebastian Bach** (1685–1750) is considered to be one of the greatest composers of all time. He lived during the Baroque era and is best known for his cantatas, many works for organ, *Magnificat*, *St. John Passion* and *St. Matthew Passion*.

Modest Petrovich Mussorgsky (1839–1881) was a Russian composer who often used his country's history and folklore to inspire his compositions, such as *Boris Godunov*, *Night on Bald Mountain* and *Pictures at an Exhibition*, which includes *The Great Gate of Kiev*.

CHORALE—*Full band arrangement. Is this a major or minor key?*

Johann Sebastian Bach

171

A **RALLENTANDO** or **RITARDANDO** is an indication that the tempo is supposed to become gradually slower. It is indicated with the abbreviation *rall.* or *rit.*

THE GREAT GATE OF KIEV—*Full band arrangement.* Pictures at an Exhibition *represents a tour through an art gallery. In addition to form and color, music uses many of the same concepts as the visual arts.*

Modest Mussorgsky

172

▶ Complete the **SOUND CHECK** near the end of your book.

Level 6: Sound Performance

A **SOLO** is a piece that is performed alone or with accompaniment. Before playing this piece, watch and listen to it being performed online.

SOLO: SCARBOROUGH FAIR—*This solo has a piano accompaniment.*

Traditional English Ballad

Piano Accompaniment

174 **THE BLUE-TAIL FLY (duet)**—*Switch parts on the repeat.*

American Minstrel Song

> A **TRIO** is a composition in which three different parts are played by three performers at the same time.
>
> Many factors go into creating a great performance. Develop a list of things you think a performer should do to prepare for a performance. You might include such things as being on time, being prepared and practicing.

175 **MOLLY MALONE (trio)**—*Learn all three parts.*

Traditional Irish Ballad

TIME TRIALS—*Count and clap this exercise before you play. This piece reviews all the meters you have learned.*

176

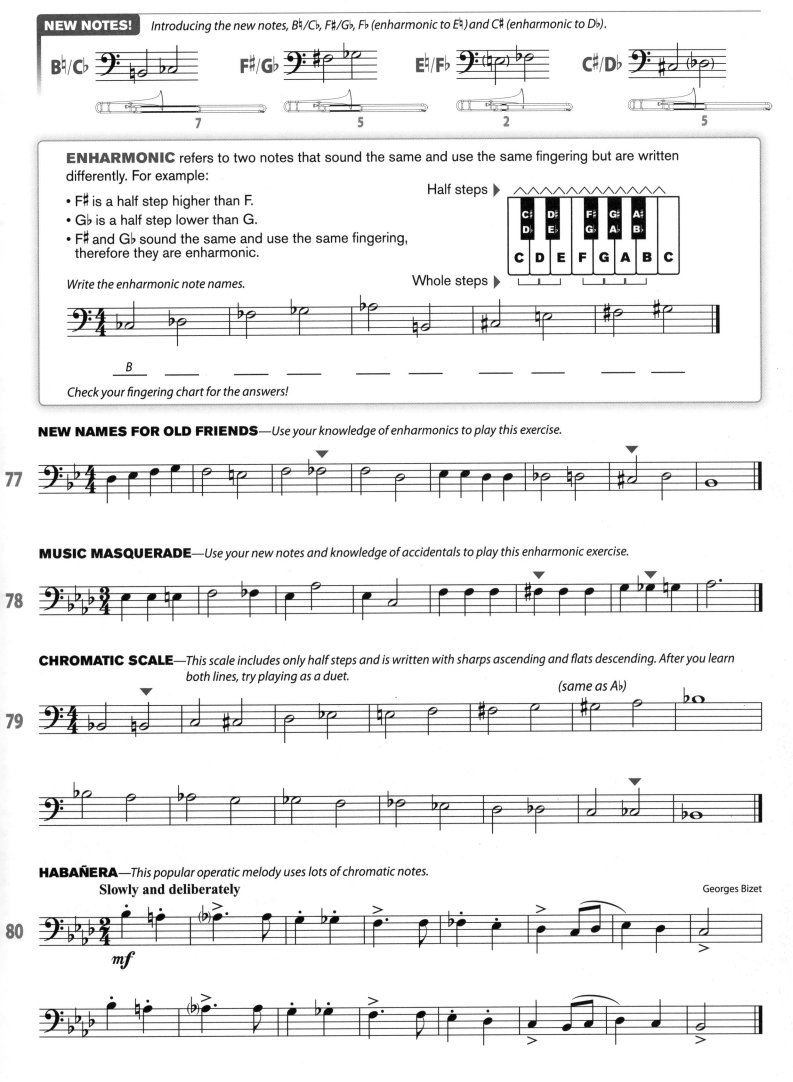

NEW NOTES! *Introducing the new notes, B♮/C♭, F♯/G♭, F♭ (enharmonic to E♮) and C♯ (enharmonic to D♭).*

ENHARMONIC refers to two notes that sound the same and use the same fingering but are written differently. For example:

- F♯ is a half step higher than F.
- G♭ is a half step lower than G.
- F♯ and G♭ sound the same and use the same fingering, therefore they are enharmonic.

Write the enharmonic note names.

Check your fingering chart for the answers!

NEW NAMES FOR OLD FRIENDS—*Use your knowledge of enharmonics to play this exercise.*

77

MUSIC MASQUERADE—*Use your new notes and knowledge of accidentals to play this enharmonic exercise.*

78

CHROMATIC SCALE—*This scale includes only half steps and is written with sharps ascending and flats descending. After you learn both lines, try playing as a duet.*

(same as A♭)

79

HABAÑERA—*This popular operatic melody uses lots of chromatic notes.*

Georges Bizet

Slowly and deliberately

80

mf

42

O CANADA—*This is the Canadian National Anthem. Play this in four-measure phrases by breathing after the long notes.*

Calixa Lavallée

181

GRANT US PEACE (round)—*Play this well-known round with the full band or as a trio.*

182

TAKE A RIDE ON THE BLUES TRAIN—*Full band arrangement. Choose from the notes provided and make up a part as you play.*
This is called **IMPROVISATION***. Your director will indicate when it is your turn to improvise.*

183

▶ Complete the **SOUND CHECK** near the end of your book.

Scales, Arpeggios, Warm-Up Chorales and Etudes*

Key of F Major

SCALE & ARPEGGIO

84

CHORALE IN CONCERT F MAJOR—*Full band arrangement.*

85

SCALE ETUDE

86

INTERVAL ETUDE

87

Key of B♭ Major

SCALE & ARPEGGIO

88

CHORALE IN CONCERT B♭ MAJOR—*Full band arrangement.*

89

SCALE ETUDE

90

INTERVAL ETUDE

91

*Scale and Etude exercises may be played with other instruments but are not always in unison.

Key of E♭ Major

SCALE & ARPEGGIO

192

CHORALE IN CONCERT E♭ MAJOR—*Full band arrangement.*

193

mf

SCALE ETUDE

194

INTERVAL ETUDE

195

Key of A♭ Major

SCALE & ARPEGGIO

196

CHORALE IN CONCERT A♭ MAJOR—*Full band arrangement.*

197

mf

SCALE ETUDE

198

INTERVAL ETUDE

199

Rhythm Studies

Sound Check

Level 1
Check off each skill you have mastered.

___ Posture   ___ Hand position

___ Instrument assembly   ___ New notes

___ New rhythms   ___ Fermata

Level 2
Check off each skill you have mastered.

___ Conducting in $\frac{2}{4}$ and $\frac{4}{4}$ time ___ Slurs

___ Playing p and f ___ New rhythms

___ New notes   ___ Breathing skills

Level 3
Check off each skill you have mastered.

___ Conducting in $\frac{3}{4}$ time   ___ Accents

___ Repeats   ___ New notes

___ Playing mp and mf ___ Pickup notes

Level 4
Check off each skill you have mastered.

___ Legato   ___ Staccato

___ Composing a piece of music ___ Understanding concert etiquette

___ Identifying major and minor keys ___ D.C. al Fine

Level 5
Check off each skill you have mastered.

___ Playing a scale   ___ Arpeggio

___ Rallentando or ritardando ___ New notes

___ Playing in a variety of styles ___ Crescendo and decrescendo (or diminuendo)

Level 6
Check off each skill you have mastered.

___ Playing a solo   ___ Playing ensembles

___ Enharmonics   ___ Chromatic scale

___ Improvisation   ___ Playing rounds

Glossary

1st and 2nd endings – play the 1st ending the first time through; repeat the music, but skip over the 1st ending on the repeat and play the 2nd ending instead

accent (>) – play the note with a strong attack

accidentals (♯, ♭, ♮) – *see page 4*

alla marcia – play in the style of a march

allegro – a fast tempo

andante – a moderate walking tempo

arpeggio – the notes of a chord played one after another

articulation – indicates how a note should be played

bass clef – indicates the fourth line of the staff is F

breath mark – tells you to take a deep breath through your mouth

chromatics – a series of notes that move in half steps

conductor – leads groups of musicians using specific hand and arm patterns

courtesy accidentals – help remind you of the key signature; occur after another accidental or recent key change; enclosed in parentheses

crescendo – gradually play louder

D.C. al Fine – repeat from the beginning and play to the *Fine*

D.S. al Fine – repeat from the sign (𝄋) and play to the *Fine*

decrescendo or diminuendo – gradually play softer

divisi – indicates where two notes appear at the same time

dot – increases the length of a note by half its value

double bar line – indicates the end of a section

duet – a composition for two performers

dynamics – change in volume

enharmonic – refers to two notes that sound the same and use the same fingering but are written differently

etude – a "study" piece, or an exercise that helps you practice a specific technique

fermata – hold a note or rest longer than its normal duration

Fine – the end of a piece of music

forte (𝆑) – play loudly

harmony – two or more notes played at the same time

improvisation – creating music as you play

interlude – a short musical piece

interval – the distance between two notes

key signature – appears at the beginning of the staff, and indicates which notes will be played sharp or flat

largo – a slow tempo

ledger line – short, horizontal line used to extend the staff either higher or lower

legato (–) – an articulation or style of playing that is smooth and connected

mezzo forte (𝆐𝆑) – medium loud

mezzo piano (𝆐𝆏) – medium soft

moderato – a medium tempo

multiple-measure rest – indicates more than one full measure of rest; the number above the staff indicates how many measures to rest

octave – the interval of an 8th

one-measure repeat (𝄎) – play the previous measure again

phrase – a musical idea that ends with a breath

piano (𝆏) – play softly

pickup note – occurs before the first complete measure of a phrase

rallentando – becoming gradually slower

rehearsal mark – reference number or letter in a box above the staff

repeat sign – go back to the beginning and play the piece again

right-facing repeat – indicates where to begin repeating the music

ritardando – becoming gradually slower

round – music in which players start the piece at different times, creating interesting harmonies and accompaniments

scale – a series of notes that ascend or descend stepwise within a key; the lowest and highest notes of the scale are always the same letter name and are an octave apart

slur – a curved line connecting two or more notes; tongue only the first note in a slur

solo – when one person is performing alone or with accompaniment

staccato (·) – an articulation or style of playing that is light and separated

style marking – sometimes used instead of a tempo marking to help musicians understand the feeling the composer would like the music to convey

syncopation – occurs when there is emphasis on a weak beat

tempo markings – indicate the speed of the music

theme and variation – a compositional technique in which the composer clearly states a melody (theme), then changes it by adding contrasting variations

tie – a curved line that connects two or more notes of the same pitch; the tied notes are played as one longer note with the combined value of both notes

time signature or meter – indicates the number of beats (counts) in each measure and the type of note that receives one beat

treble clef – indicates the second line of the staff is G

trio – a composition in which three different parts are played by three performers at the same time

tutti – everyone plays together

unison – two or more parts play the same note

waltz – a popular dance in $\frac{3}{4}$ time

Trombone Slide Position Chart

This diagram indicates where the top of the slide is located in each position.

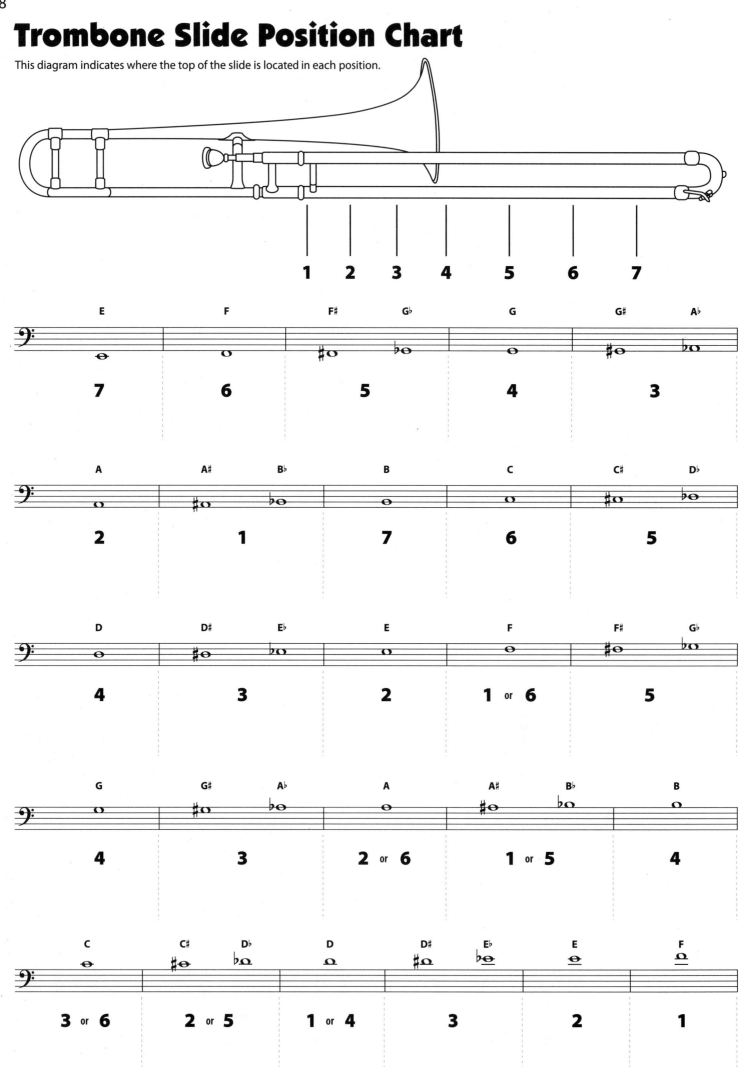

THERE'S A NIGHTMARE
IN MY CLOSET

written and illustrated by Mercer Mayer

Dial Books for Young Readers
New York

Marianna

From cotton to rabbit

There used to be a nightmare in my closet.

Before going to sleep,

I always closed the closet door.

I was even afraid to turn around and look.

When I was safe in bed, I'd peek...

sometimes.

One night I decided to get rid of my nightmare
once and for all.

As soon as the room was dark, I heard
him creeping toward me.

Quickly I turned on the light and caught him sitting at the foot of my bed.

"Go away, Nightmare, or I'll shoot you," I said.

I shot him anyway.

My nightmare began to cry.

I was mad...

but not too mad.

"Nightmare, be quiet or you'll wake
Mommy and Daddy," I said.

He wouldn't stop crying so I took
him by the hand

and tucked him in bed

and closed the closet door.

I suppose there's another nightmare in my
closet, but my bed's not big enough for three.